Close-up Continents

Mapping Europe

Paul Rockett

✦

with artwork by Mark Ruffle

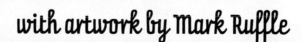

W

FRANKLIN WATTS

Franklin Watts
First published in Great Britain in 2016
by The Watts Publishing Group

Executive editor: Adrian Cole
Series design and illustration: Mark Ruffle
www.rufflebrothers.com

Picture credits:
Ace Stock/Alamy: 25br; Dcoetzee/CC
Wikimedia: 26bl; A Howden International/
Alamy: 25bl; Pavel Konovalov/Dreamstime:
19bl; Lukiyanova Natalia/frenta/
Shutterstock: 19br; Supergenijalac/
Dreamstime: 21tc; CC Wikimedia: 4c, 6-7;
Rob Wilson/Shutterstock: 21tr.

Dewey number: 914
ISBN: 978 1 4451 4108 4

Printed in Malaysia

Franklin Watts
An imprint of Hachette Children's Group
Part of The Watts Publishing Group
Carmelite House
50 Victoria Embankment
London EC4Y 0DZ

An Hachette UK Company.
www.hachette.co.uk

www.franklinwatts.co.uk

Contents

Where is Europe? ·········· 4
Countries ·········· 6
Dividing and uniting Europe ·········· 8
Regions of Europe ·········· 10
Climates ·········· 12
Wildlife ·········· 14
Natural landmarks ·········· 16
Manmade landmarks ·········· 18
Industry ·········· 20
Mapping capital cities ·········· 22
Sport ·········· 24
Culture ·········· 26
Food and drink ·········· 28
Further information ·········· 30
Glossary ·········· 31
Index ·········· 32

Where is Europe?

Europe is part of a giant landmass that borders Asia, and includes a small number of islands in surrounding seas and oceans. Many early maps were made by European adventurers who travelled beyond the continent, 'discovering' new lands.

European map-making

This is one of the first maps of the world. It was created in 1482 in Germany, following instructions that were originally written in 150 CE, by a Greek astronomer, Ptolemy.

What does a map do?

Maps show you where things are and can be used to help you get from one place to another. They can also show you the distance between two places, but the map needs to be accurate and to scale.

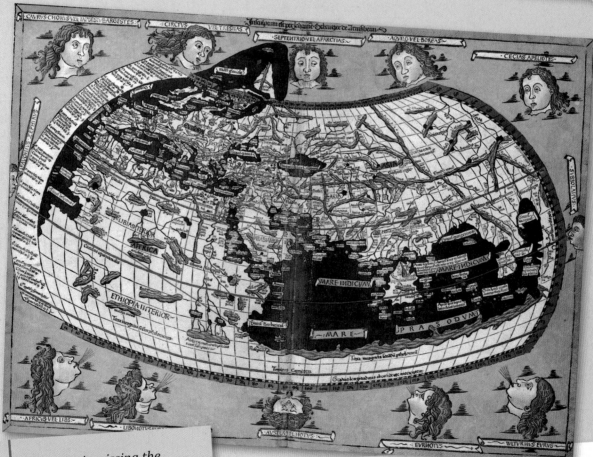

This map is missing the continents of North and South America, Australasia and Antarctica. These are places that had yet to be visited by Europeans.

During the 1400s and 1500s European explorers set out to find new routes across the seas to Asia, encountering unknown countries that they recorded on maps.

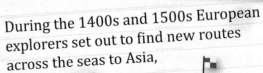

Latitude and longitude

World maps feature a grid of imaginary lines called latitude and longitude. These lines are numbered so that places can be located using the number of the latitude line first, followed by the number of the longitude line.

Lines of latitude go round the world from east to west. The Equator is a line of latitude (0°).

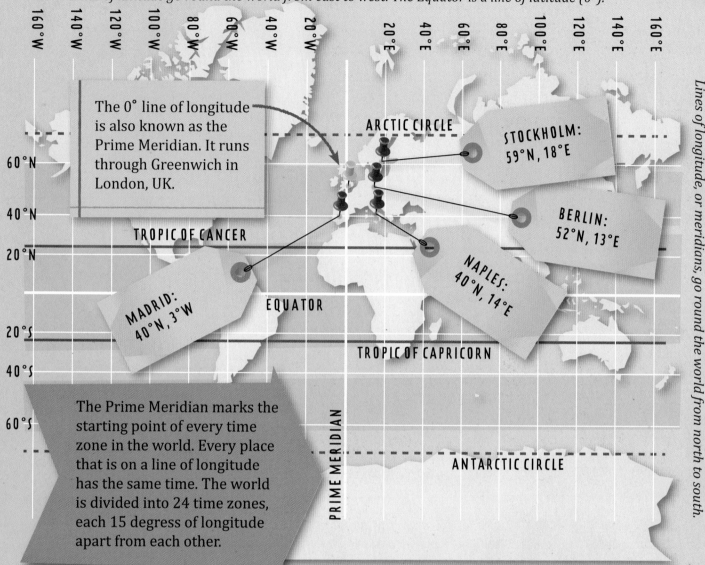

The 0° line of longitude is also known as the Prime Meridian. It runs through Greenwich in London, UK.

STOCKHOLM: 59°N, 18°E

BERLIN: 52°N, 13°E

NAPLES: 40°N, 14°E

MADRID: 40°N, 3°W

ARCTIC CIRCLE

TROPIC OF CANCER

EQUATOR

TROPIC OF CAPRICORN

ANTARCTIC CIRCLE

PRIME MERIDIAN

The Prime Meridian marks the starting point of every time zone in the world. Every place that is on a line of longitude has the same time. The world is divided into 24 time zones, each 15 degress of longitude apart from each other.

Lines of longitude, or meridians, go round the world from north to south.

What surrounds Europe?

You can use a map to locate a place by using grid references, such as lines of latitude and longitude. You can also describe a place in relation to the compass points of north, east, south or west.

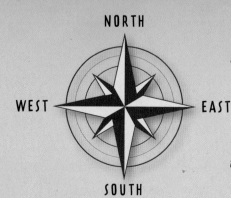

North of Europe is the Arctic Ocean

To the west of Europe is the Atlantic Ocean

Asia is east of Europe

To the south of Europe is the Mediterranean Sea

Africa is south of Europe

Countries

Europe may be the second smallest continent, but it has the third largest population of around 742.5 million people.

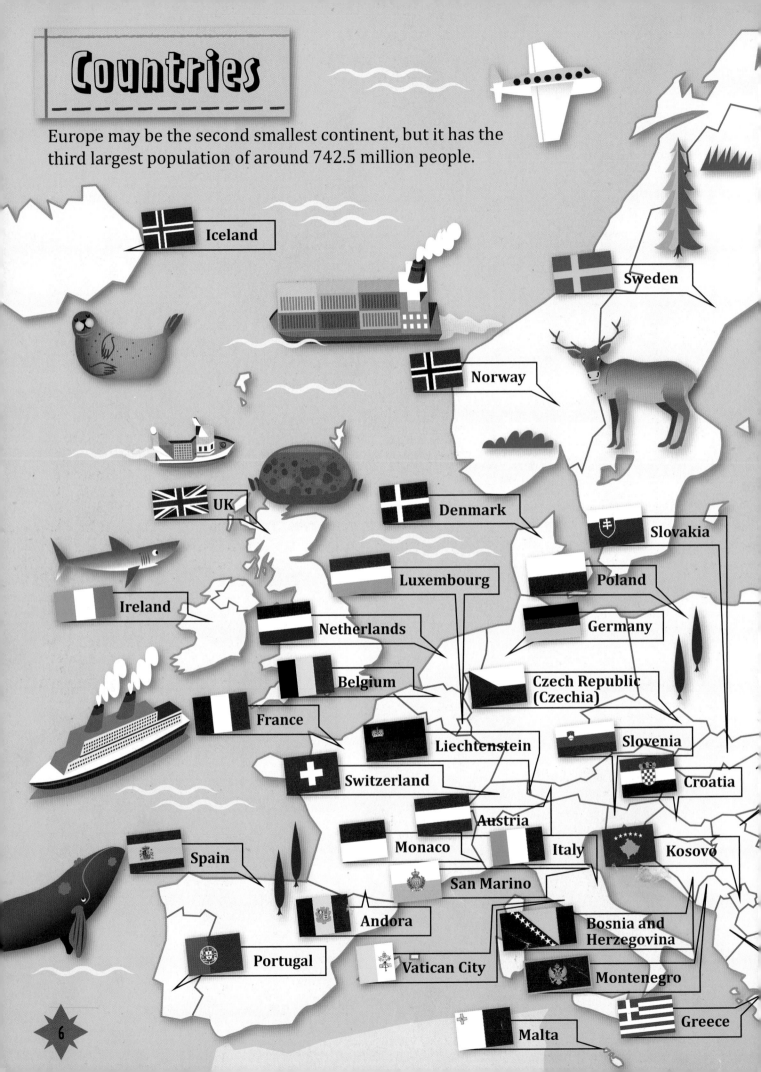

- Iceland
- Sweden
- Norway
- UK
- Denmark
- Slovakia
- Luxembourg
- Poland
- Ireland
- Netherlands
- Germany
- Belgium
- Czech Republic (Czechia)
- France
- Liechtenstein
- Slovenia
- Switzerland
- Croatia
- Austria
- Monaco
- Italy
- Kosovo
- Spain
- San Marino
- Andora
- Bosnia and Herzegovina
- Portugal
- Vatican City
- Montenegro
- Malta
- Greece

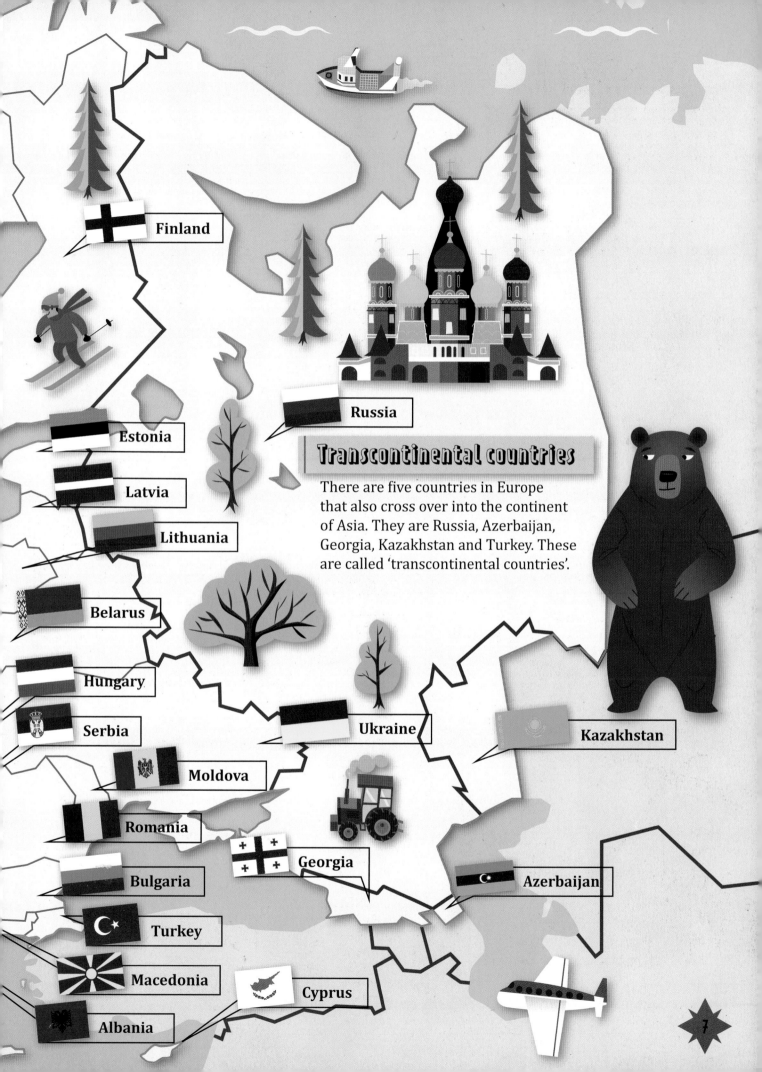

Finland

Estonia

Latvia

Lithuania

Belarus

Hungary

Serbia

Moldova

Romania

Bulgaria

Turkey

Macedonia

Albania

Russia

Transcontinental countries

There are five countries in Europe that also cross over into the continent of Asia. They are Russia, Azerbaijan, Georgia, Kazakhstan and Turkey. These are called 'transcontinental countries'.

Ukraine

Kazakhstan

Georgia

Azerbaijan

Cyprus

Dividing and uniting Europe

The Europe we know today is different from the Europe that existed 25 years ago and even more unrecognisable from that of 10,000 years ago. The number of countries and their borders have changed throughout history.

20th century Europe

During the 20th century, the map of Europe, particularly in the East, went through many changes.

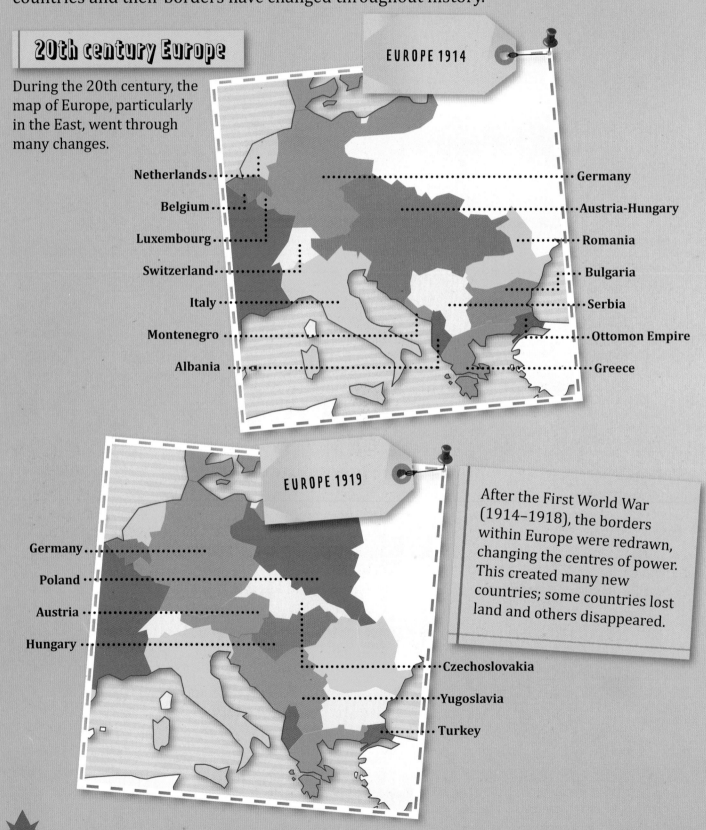

EUROPE 1914

- Netherlands
- Belgium
- Luxembourg
- Switzerland
- Italy
- Montenegro
- Albania
- Germany
- Austria-Hungary
- Romania
- Bulgaria
- Serbia
- Ottomon Empire
- Greece

EUROPE 1919

- Germany
- Poland
- Austria
- Hungary
- Czechoslovakia
- Yugoslavia
- Turkey

After the First World War (1914–1918), the borders within Europe were redrawn, changing the centres of power. This created many new countries; some countries lost land and others disappeared.

After the Second World War (1939–1945), Germany was divided into two countries: East Germany and West Germany. In 1961, a wall was built splitting the capital city, Berlin, in two. One half belonged to communist East Germany, and the other half to democratic West Germany.

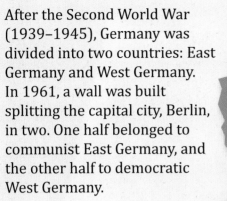

GERMANY

WEST

EAST

BERLIN WALL

In 1989 the Berlin Wall came down, and not long after East and West Germany were reunited as one country. This moment led to a gradual change of politics in Eastern Europe.

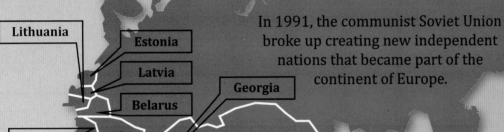

Russia

In 1991, the communist Soviet Union broke up creating new independent nations that became part of the continent of Europe.

Lithuania

Estonia

Latvia

Belarus

Georgia

Moldova

Ukraine

Azerbaijan

Kazakhstan

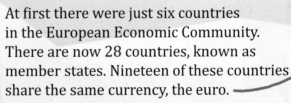

The European Union

Although each country within Europe has its own government and parliament, some seek to work together as part of a group called the European Union (EU). The member states work together to help each other with political and economic problems.

At first there were just six countries in the European Economic Community. There are now 28 countries, known as member states. Nineteen of these countries share the same currency, the euro.

The EU is made up of the following countries:

Year they joined the EU	Countries					
1957	Belgium	France	Germany	Italy	Luxembourg	Netherlands
1973	Denmark	Ireland	United Kingdom			
1981	Greece					
1986	Portugal	Spain				
1995	Austria	Finland	Sweden			
2004	Cyprus	Czech Republic	Estonia	Hungary	Latvia	Lithuania
	Poland	Slovakia	Malta	Slovenia		
2007	Bulgaria	Romania				
2013	Croatia					

Regions of Europe

When people talk about Europe, they often divide it up into regions. The regions are connected by their location and often share a similar history and language. The four main points of the compass are used to split Europe into four regions: Northern Europe, Eastern Europe, Southern Europe and Western Europe.

Greenland

Northern Europe ○

Northern Europe is made up of the following countries: Iceland, Norway, Sweden, Finland, Denmark, the United Kingdom, Ireland, Estonia, Latvia and Lithuania.

British Isles

The British Isles refers to a collection of islands. It includes the United Kingdom and Ireland, and although it has the word 'British' in its title, it does not describe a collective nationality.

The United Kingdom is made up of Northern Ireland, Scotland, Wales and England, whereas Great Britain refers to just Scotland, Wales and England.

Western Europe ○

The countries of Western Europe are: France, Germany, Austria, Belgium, Liechtenstein, Monaco, Netherlands, Luxembourg and Switzerland.

Southern Europe ○

Southern Europe is made up of countries that border with the Mediterranean Sea as well as those further inland that share a warm Mediterranean climate (see pages 12–13).

Nordic countries

The Nordic countries include Denmark, Finland, Iceland, Norway, Sweden and Greenland. Greenland is part of the North American continent, but is also part of the Kingdom of Denmark. It used to be governed by the Danish, and still shares many political and cultural similarities with its former ruler.

Scandinavia

The countries of Norway, Sweden and Denmark are known collectively as Scandinavia. They share a common history. In the past, these countries fought each other over their territories, and the people who lived in these countries were known as Vikings.

Baltic states

The three countries, Latvia, Estonia and Lithuania, are often referred to as the Baltics. The name comes from the Baltic Sea, with these countries sitting on its eastern coast.

Benelux

Benelux is a region that unites Belgium, Netherlands and Luxembourg. These countries established Benelux as a union in 1944. The name is made up of the initial letters of each country: *Be*lgium, *Ne*therlands, *Lux*embourg. They are also referred to as the Low Countries, as much of their land is flat and below sea level.

Eastern Europe

Eastern Europe is made up of Poland, the Czech Republic, Hungary, Romania, Bulgaria and the countries that are east of these. These countries have histories that connect them to the Soviet Union (see page 9). Some people include the Baltic States in this region.

Climates

Europe can be divided up into four different climate zones:
Mediterranean ○
marine west coast ○
humid continental ○
subarctic ○
Each zone experiences different temperatures and weather conditions that shape their wildlife and the lifestyles of people who live there.

Subarctic zone

The subarctic climate is cold and snowy with very long winters and short mild summers, lasting from one to three months. The very north of this zone falls into the Arctic Circle, where the ground is permanently frozen, making it difficult for plants, other than mosses and lichen, to grow.

Humid continental zone

The climate in Europe's humid continental zone varies between the four seasons, as it does across Europe. But it is here that the differences are felt most strongly.

SPRING	SUMMER	AUTUMN	WINTER
warm and wet	warm and humid	cool and dry	cold and harsh

Marine west coast zone

The marine west coast climate zone is in the path of westerly ocean winds. These winds bring cloudy skies and keep the air over the land cool in summer and mild in the winter.

Mediterranean zone

The Mediterranean climate is known for long, hot and dry summers and cool, wet winters. The mountain ranges further inland block out the cold north winds, while hot, steady winds blow in from Africa.

Isotherms

Maps are used to show weather forecasts and can be used to give us an overview of how weather differs across areas of land.
This isotherm map on the right shows the average temperature in January. Each line (isotherm) crosses over an area that has the same temperature.

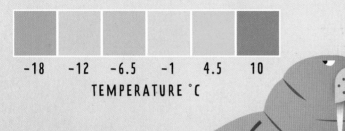

−18	−12	−6.5	−1	4.5	10

TEMPERATURE °C

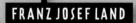

FRANZ JOSEF LAND

Northernmost point

At the northernmost part of Europe is an archipelago, called Franz Josef Land that is part of Russia. It's made up of 191 islands, which are mainly covered in sheets of ice. It's an unwelcome home for humans, but a perfect sanctuary for Arctic wildlife such as walruses. It has a record low temperature of -44.4°C.

Wettest place

Crkvice, in the mountains of Montenegro, is the wettest inhabited place in Europe. It's within the Mediterranean climate and remains dry during summer but pours with rain during the rest of the year. Its average annual rainfall is around 4,648 mm, hitting a record 8,036 mm in 1937.

CRKVICE

ALMERÍA

GAVDOS

Southernmost point

At the southernmost part of Europe is a Greek island called Gavdos. This small island is a popular destination for tourists looking for beaches and hot weather. In the summer temperatures can reach above 40°C.

JULY

JANUARY

AVERAGE TEMPERATURE °C

SOUTHERNMOST EUROPE	
NORTHERNMOST EUROPE	

Driest place

Almería, in southern Spain, is the driest city in Europe. It only experiences around 26 days of rain per year, with an average annual rainfall of just 196 mm.

13

Wildlife

Europe has a huge range of wildlife, from polar bears in the Arctic to sand snakes in the Mediterranean. Over thousands of years, humans have cut down forests and woodlands, which now only cover about 25 per cent of the continent. However, in some of these forests you can still see bears and boars, and ancient oak trees.

Arctic fox

Peregrine falcon

European elk

Polar bear

Grey seal

European squid

Wolverine

Atlantic cod

Atlantic cod can be found in the waters around Iceland, Norway and the UK. It is one of the world's most popular fish to eat, particularly in the UK, Spain and Portugal.

English oak

Tulips

Wild boar

Pine marten

Iberian lynx

The Iberian lynx is one of the most endangered species of animal in Europe, with only around 300 living in the wild. Its habitat in Spain and Portugal has been reduced through the construction of roads and towns, and its diet of rabbit has been affected by a series of diseases.

Gallic rooster

Nettle-tree butterfly

Asp viper

Olive tree

Bottlenose dolphin

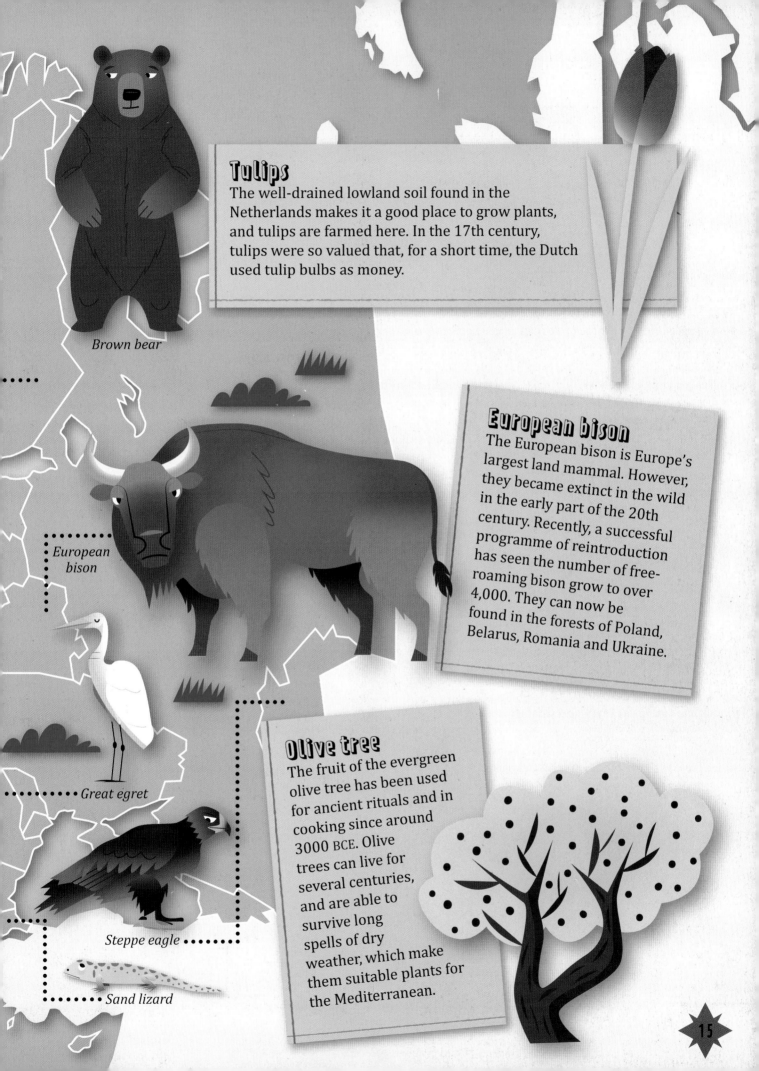

Brown bear

Tulips
The well-drained lowland soil found in the Netherlands makes it a good place to grow plants, and tulips are farmed here. In the 17th century, tulips were so valued that, for a short time, the Dutch used tulip bulbs as money.

European bison

European bison
The European bison is Europe's largest land mammal. However, they became extinct in the wild in the early part of the 20th century. Recently, a successful programme of reintroduction has seen the number of free-roaming bison grow to over 4,000. They can now be found in the forests of Poland, Belarus, Romania and Ukraine.

Great egret

Olive tree
The fruit of the evergreen olive tree has been used for ancient rituals and in cooking since around 3000 BCE. Olive trees can live for several centuries, and are able to survive long spells of dry weather, which make them suitable plants for the Mediterranean.

Steppe eagle

Sand lizard

Natural landmarks

Between the ragged western coastlines and the towering mountain border to the east, Europe is dotted and lined with forests and rivers, and an array of natural wonders.

Fjords, Norway

Fjords are long, narrow inlets of water with steep walls of rock on either side. Huge slow-moving glaciers carved out the deep fjords. There are more fjords in Norway than anywhere else in the world.••••••••

Giant's Causeway

Giant's Causeway is a natural rock formation of around 40,000 interlocking basalt columns. Most of the columns are hexagonal, and some are as high as 11.8 m.

The Irish legend about a giant called Finn McCool tells how he built the causeway to cross over to Scotland to fight another giant. In fact, the causeway was created around 60 million years ago as a result of a volcanic eruption. The lava cooled quickly, forming the distinctive basalt shapes.

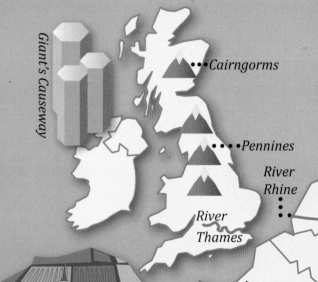

Giant's Causeway

•••*Cairngorms*

•••*Pennines*

River Rhine

River Thames

River Seine

River Loire •••

River Rhône •••

Pyrenees

Auvergne Mountains•••••••••

The Auvergne Mountains are the highest peaks in the Massif Central, an area that is covered with dense forests and extinct volcanoes covered in greenery.

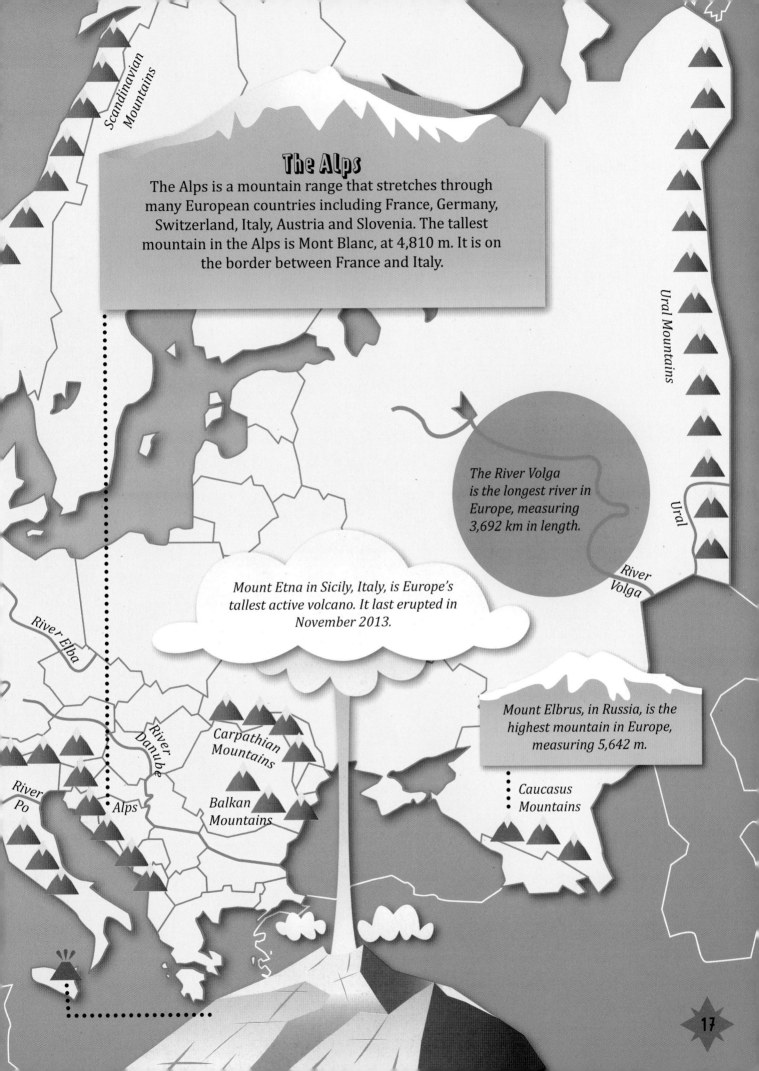

The Alps

The Alps is a mountain range that stretches through many European countries including France, Germany, Switzerland, Italy, Austria and Slovenia. The tallest mountain in the Alps is Mont Blanc, at 4,810 m. It is on the border between France and Italy.

Scandinavian Mountains

Ural Mountains

The River Volga is the longest river in Europe, measuring 3,692 km in length.

Ural

River Volga

Mount Etna in Sicily, Italy, is Europe's tallest active volcano. It last erupted in November 2013.

River Elba

Mount Elbrus, in Russia, is the highest mountain in Europe, measuring 5,642 m.

River Danube

Carpathian Mountains

Caucasus Mountains

River Po

Alps

Balkan Mountains

Manmade landmarks

From classical columns to giant glass shards, Europe has been a leading force in architecture throughout history. Each country is filled with buildings designed to withstand enemy attacks, for worship and as grand displays of power, wealth and industry.

Hagia Sophia

The Hagia Sophia, in Istanbul in Turkey, was built between 532 and 537. It was originally a church, then converted into a mosque and is now a museum. It's a space that inspires awe and worship.

Great Belt Bridge

Measuring 6.79 km in length, the Great Belt Bridge is one of the longest bridges in the world. It connects the Danish islands of Funen and Zealand.

Parthenon

The Parthenon, built between 447–432 BCE, sits atop the Acropolis ('high city') in Athens, and stands as a symbol of ancient Greek order and wealth.

Caerphilly Castle

There are over 500 castles in Wales, UK. That's more castles per head than anywhere else in the world. Caerphilly Castle, built in the 13th century, is the largest castle in Wales.

Atomium

The Atomium in Belgium looks like an iron crystal magnified 165 billion times. It was built in 1958 for the Brussels World Fair.

Alhambra

For around 800 years Moorish monarchs (Muslims from North Africa), ruled parts of Spain. They built the Alhambra in Granada between the 9th and 13th centuries. It was later converted into a palace. It contains stunning pieces of Moorish artwork and architecture.

TURNING TORSO

SAINT BASIL'S CATHEDRAL

WINDMILLS AT KINDERDIJK

STONEHENGE

EIFFEL TOWER

Italian architecture

Italy is packed with buildings covering almost 3,000 years of history and many different styles of architecture.

Colosseum

The colosseum was the largest amphitheatre in the Roman Empire. It was built in 80 BCE and could hold around 50,000 spectators. They came to watch gladiators fight each other or fight wild animals.

Pompeii

When the volcano, Mount Vesuvius, erupted in 79 CE it buried the nearby town of Pompeii under large piles of ash. The town was rediscovered in the 16th century and archaeologists have been uncovering the city's remains ever since.

PIRELLI TOWER, 1950S, MILAN

SAINT MARK'S CATHEDRAL, 832–1094, VENICE

CATHEDRAL OF SAINT MARY OF THE FLOWER, 1296–1436, FLORENCE

POMPEII

VALLEY OF THE TEMPLES, 6TH CENTURY BCE, AGRIGENTO, SICILY

COLISEUM

LEANING TOWER OF PISA, 1173–1372, PISA

CRESPI'S CASTLE, 1890S, CAPRIATE SAN GERVASIO

NECROPOLIS OF THE BANDITACCIA, 9TH–3RD CENTURY BCE, CERVETERI

Industry

Europe is a continent with a wide variety of industries, including farming, manufacturing and tourism. Large networks of pipes and power stations are spread out over the land and in the sea, supplying the energy needed to keep these industries running.

Main industries in Europe

Crops:
- Barley
- Fruit
- Corn
- Oats
- Rye
- Wheat
- Vineyards

Industry:
- Manufacturing/ industrial areas
- Car industry
- Forestry
- Hi-tech
- Fishing
- Tourism

Livestock:
- Cattle
- Sheep
- Pigs

Tourism and France

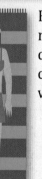

France is the world's most popular tourist destination. Over 10 per cent of the population work in tourism.

More people visit France each year than live in the country! France offers visitors sunny beaches, snowy mountains for skiing and a long rich history to retrace.

Cars

The car industry is a major employer and contributor of wealth to many countries in Europe, particularly Germany, France, Italy and the Czech Republic.

The largest producer of cars in Europe is Germany. Around six million cars are made in Germany each year and five million are produced overseas in German-owned factories. World-famous and popular car brands from Germany include Volkswagen, BMW, Porsche and Mercedes-Benz.

Natural resources

GERMAN CARS ARE POPULAR ALL AROUND THE WORLD.

We need a supply of energy resources to generate the power that keeps factories manufacturing and the farm tractors running – as well as providing electricity in the home. Different countries in Europe rely on different energy sources; some have plenty of their own, whereas others have to rely on imports.

Energy:
- **O** OIL
- NATURAL GAS
- HYDROELECTRICITY
- COAL
- NUCLEAR

Natural gas

Natural gas is a fossil fuel, created from dead animals and plants buried deep underground that have rotted over millions of years. Like the other fossil fuels – coal and oil – we burn gas to generate electricity.

Russia has the largest reserve of natural gas and is Europe's biggest supplier. The gas is delivered through large underground and undersea pipes.

Mapping capital cities

Histories of conflict and trade have shaped many of Europe's capital cities. Many have been built around centres of power, such as royal palaces or government buildings, as well as large rivers that have provided vital routes for transporting goods.

The capital of Russia is Moscow, and at the centre of this city sits the Kremlin. The name Kremlin means 'fortress inside a city', and inside the Kremlin in Moscow are government buildings, towers and palaces. Nearby is Saint Basil's Cathedral and Red Square, where the main streets of Moscow begin.

Moscow

Saint Basil's Cathedral

The Great Kremlin Palace

Red Square

Paris

Paris, the capital of France, was rebuilt between 1852 and 1870 with wide streets, parks and squares. This was to allow more space for vehicles to get through, but also to prevent people from forming barricades across the streets to protest, causing disruptions.

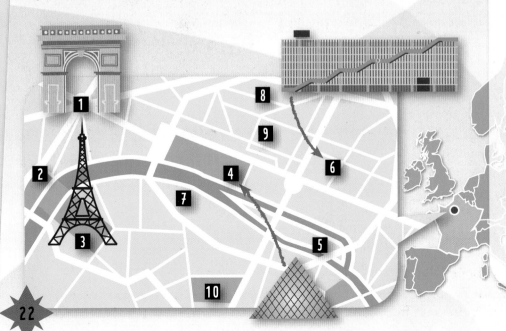

PARIS TOURIST SPOTS:

1 Arc de Triomphe
2 Palais de Chaillot
3 Eiffel Tower
4 Louvre
5 Notre Dame
6 Pompidou Centre
7 Musée d'Orsay
8 Opéra
9 Palais Royal
10 Palais du Luxembourg

Stockholm

The city of Stockholm, the capital of Sweden, is unusual in that it is built around fourteen islands. The central island, Stadsholmen, also known as the Old Town, is where the Royal Palace sits.

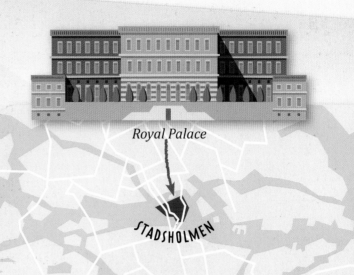

Royal Palace

STADSHOLMEN

The islands are connected by bridges. However during cold winters the surrounding waters freeze over, making it possible for people to walk in between some of the islands on the ice.

Budapest

Budapest, the capital of Hungary, used to be two cities: Buda, to the west of the River Danube, and Pest, to the east of the river.

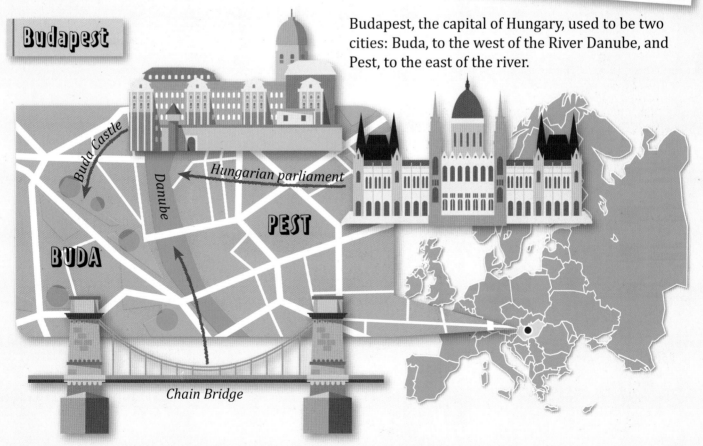

Buda Castle

Danube

Hungarian parliament

PEST

BUDA

Chain Bridge

In 1849, the Chain Bridge was opened; it linked both cities and was the first permanent bridge across the River Danube. However, it wasn't until 1873 that Buda and Pest were officially merged, becoming Budapest.

Sport

Balls, wheels, rackets and skis are just a few of the items used for sporting tournaments in Europe. Competitions are played at local, national, continental and international levels.

Tour de France

The world's most famous bike race is the Tour de France. In July each year, teams of male cyclists attempt to cover 3,000-plus km in three weeks.

The route changes each year, sometimes passing through different countries, but it always goes through the Alps and Pyrenées and finishes on the Champs-Élysées in Paris.

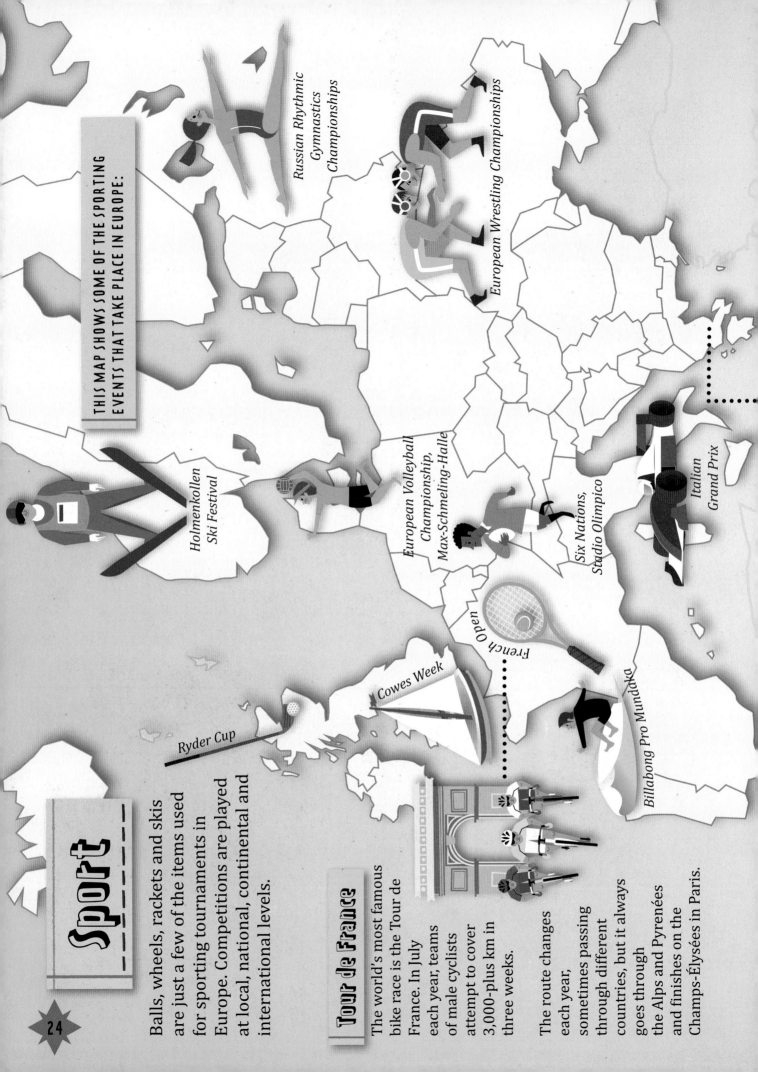

Russian Rhythmic Gymnastics Championships

European Wrestling Championships

Holmenkollen Ski Festival

European Volleyball Championship, Max-Schmeling-Halle

Six Nations, Stadio Olimpico

Italian Grand Prix

French Open

Cowes Week

Ryder Cup

Billabong Pro Mundaka

Football

Football is by far the most popular sport in Europe. Each country has its own national team that takes part in major international football tournaments. This includes the UEFA European Championships. This event takes place every four years in a different European country. Spain and Germany have both won three times – more than any other country.

Past winners of the UEFA European Championships:

YEAR	LOCATION	WINNER
1996	England	Germany
2000	Netherlands	France
2004	Portugal	Greece
2008	Austria	Spain
2012	Ukraine	Spain
2016	France	?

The Olympic Games

The Olympic Games is the biggest international sporting event in the world. It takes place every four years, with countries from all over the world taking part in more than 90 different competitions.

The first ancient Olympic Games was held in Olympia in Greece in 776 BCE, with Greek-only sportsmen. The ancient Games included running, long jump, javelin, boxing and chariot races.

The first modern Olympic Games, similar to what we know today, was held in Athens in 1896.

This ancient Greek vase shows Olympic runners.

The opening ceremony from the 2012 London Olympic Games.

Culture

Europe has blazed a trail in the art world for centuries, producing ground-breaking literature, art, music and dance. Its rich culture has been influenced by religious beliefs, ancient ideas and developments in technology, all spreading out across the continent.

William Shakespeare

William Shakespeare was a poet and playwright, born in Stratford-upon-Avon in 1564. He wrote a total of 37 plays, some of which explore people and moments from history, while others are romances, comedies and tragedies. His most famous plays include *Romeo and Juliet* and *Hamlet*.

Shakespeare's plays are performed all around the world, with many people considering him to be the greatest writer in the English language.

The Renaissance

The Renaissance was a period in European history, from the 14th–16th century, that saw artists and scientists explore ideas from ancient Greece and Rome. It saw an explosion of new talent that influenced a change in culture, education and technology. The centre for Renaissance art was Italy, where techniques in painting and sculpture looked for new ways to represent the world.

The Mona Lisa *(1503–17) is a Renaissance painting by Leonardo da Vinci (1452–1519).*

Stratford-upon-Avon

River Danube

Rome

The headquarters of the Catholic Church is Vatican City, a small country inside Rome, the capital of Italy. Vatican City is built around the Pope's residence, St Peter's Basilica.

Waltz

The waltz is a dance that was very popular in Vienna, Austria from early 19th century, then spreading to the rest of Europe. In the dance, partners hold each other close and glide elegantly around the dance floor.

Austrian composer Johann Strauss wrote a famous waltz called 'The Blue Danube', named after the River Danube that passes through ten European countries including Romania, Hungary, Austria and Germany.

Religion

Christianity is the largest religion in Europe and has been practised here since the 1st century CE. It's made up of different groups, such as Protestantism, Eastern Orthodoxy and Catholicism. The Catholic Church has the largest number of Christian followers in Europe. It has had a big influence over how countries have been ruled as well as the arts they have produced.

In the southeastern countries of Albania, Azerbaijan, Kosovo and Turkey, the majority of the population are Muslims. Here culture is greatly influence by the religious teachings of Islam.

Istanbul

The Sultan Ahmed Mosque, also known as the Blue Mosque, is in the capital of Turkey, Istanbul. It's filled with chandeliers, wall panels and stained glass windows with designs inspired by verses from the Qur'an.

Food and drink

Europe is a continent united by a passion for food and drink. Many countries have their own national dishes, and regions have a strong sense of loyalty to their home-grown cooking and produce.

Parma

Parma ham

ITALY

Thin slices of dry-cured ham have been produced in Parma for over two thousand years. The pigs used to make the ham must be bred in the northern and central regions of Italy. There are currently over 150 firms in Parma producing Parma ham.

Champagne

Sparkling wine that is called Champagne should have been produced in the Champagne region of France. Not all wine producers follow this rule, and legal efforts are made by the producers in the Champagne region to protect the name of their drink.

FRANCE

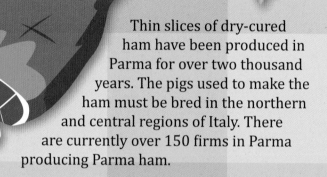

SCOTLAND

Haggis

A national food of Scotland is the haggis, a large sausage made from a sheep's stomach stuffed with chopped sheep's lungs, liver and heart, oatmeal, onion, suet (animal fat) and spices.

Ruskie pierogi

Ruskie pierogi is a traditional Polish dumpling filled with potato, cheese and onion. It comes from a region once known as Red Ruthenia, an area that today lies in both present-day Poland and Ukraine, but was once part of Poland.

Swiss chocolate

Switzerland is famous for producing high-quality chocolate – even though the main ingredient, the cacao bean, comes from thousands of kilometres away. It was at a factory in Vevey that milk chocolate was first invented, back in the late 1870s.

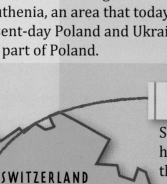

SWITZERLAND

Vevey

Cheese

Cheese is a popular food eaten all over Europe, and there are many different types. Each country, and many regions within these countries, have a make of cheese that is special to the area.

COUNTRY	FAMOUS CHEESE	
Italy	Mozzarella di bufala	
Britain	Blue Stilton	
France	Brie de Melun	
Switzerland	Gruyère	
Spain	Roncal	
Greece	Feta	
Netherlands	Edam	
Cyprus	Halloumi	
Denmark	Danish blue	
Norway	Jarlsberg	

COUNTRY	SIZE SQ KM	POPULATION	CAPITAL CITY	MAIN LANGUAGES
Russia	17,098,242 [including Asian territory]	142,470,272 [whole country]	Moscow	Russian
Turkey	783,562 [including Asian territory]	81,619,392 [whole country]	Ankara	Turkish
Germany	357,022	80,996,685	Berlin	German
France	551,500	66,259,012	Paris	French
UK	243,610	63,742,977	London	English
Italy	301,340	61,680,122	Rome	Italian
Spain	505,370	47,737,941	Madrid	Spanish
Ukraine	603,550	44,291,413	Kiev	Ukrainian
Poland	312,685	38,346,279	Warsaw	Polish
Romania	238,391	21,729,871	Bucharest	Romanian
Kazakhstan	2,724,900 [including Asian territory]	17,948,816 [whole country]	Astana	Kazakh, Russian
Netherlands	41,543	16,877,351	Amsterdam	Dutch
Portugal	92,090	10,813,834	Lisbon	Portuguese
Greece	131,957	10,775,557	Athens	Greek
Czech Republic	78,867	10,627,448	Prague	Czech
Belgium	30,528	10,449,361	Brussels	Dutch, French, German
Hungary	93,028	9,919,128	Budapest	Hungarian
Sweden	450,295	9,723,809	Stockholm	Swedish
Azerbaijan	86,600 [including Asian territory]	9,686,210 [whole country]	Baku	Azerbaijani
Belarus	207, 600	9,608,058	Minsk	Belarussian, Russian
Austria	83,871	8,223,062	Vienna	German
Switzerland	41,277	8,061,516	Bern	French, German, Italian
Serbia	77,474	7,209,764	Belgrade	Serbian
Bulgaria	110,879	6,924,716	Sofia	Bulgarian
Denmark	43,094	5,569,077	Copenhagen	Danish
Slovakia	49,035	5,443,583	Bratislava	Slovak
Finland	338,145	5,268,799	Helsinki	Finnish, Swedish
Norway	323, 802	5,147,792	Oslo	Norwegian
Georgia	69,700 [including Asian territory]	4,935,880 [whole country]	Tbilisi	Georgian
Ireland	70,273	4,832,765	Dublin	Irish, English
Croatia	56,594	4,470,534	Zagreb	Croatian
Bosnia and Herzegovina	51,197	3,871,643	Sarajevo	Bosnian
Moldova	33,851	3,583,288	Chisinau	Romanian
Lithuania	65,300	3,505,738	Vilnius	Lithuanian
Albania	28,748	3,020,209	Tirana	Albanian
Latvia	64,589	2,165,165	Riga	Latvian
Macedonia	25,713	2,091,719	Skopje	Macedonian
Slovenia	20,273	1,988,292	Ljubljana	Slovene
Kosovo	10,887	1,859,203	Pristina	Albanian, Serbian
Estonia	45,228	1,257,921	Tallinn	Estonian
Cyprus	9,251	1,172,458	Nicosia	Greek, Turkish
Montenegro	13,812	650,036	Podgorica	Montenegrin
Luxembourg	2,586	520,672	Luxembourg	Luxembourgish, French, German
Malta	316	412,655	Vallette	Maltese, English
Iceland	103,000	317,351	Reykjavik	Icelandic
Andorra	468	85,458	Andorra La Vella	Catalan
Liechtenstein	160	37,313	Vaduz	German
San Marino	61	32,742	San Marino	Italian
Monaco	2	30,508	Monaco	French
Vatican City	0.44	842	Vatican City	Italian

Glossary

amphitheatre
an open, circular building with a central space for events surrounded by an area for spectators

archipelago
a cluster of islands contained within an area of sea

astronomer
a person who studies the stars, planets and other objects in space

barricades
barriers built across streets to prevent people from passing through

basalt
dark rock formed by volcanic activity

climate
average weather conditions in a particular area

communist
a person, institution or country that supports communism, where the means of production are owned by everyone and not individuals

currency
a form of money used in different countries and continents, such as the euro or the US dollar

democratic
a form of government where the members of government have been voted in by the country's citizens

endangered
at risk of extinction

Equator
an imaginary line drawn around the Earth separating the Northern and Southern hemispheres

fossil fuel
fuel made up of the remains of living things that have been compacted underground for thousands of years (oil, gas, coal)

glacier
a mass of ice that moves slowly over a large area of land

isotherm
a line on a map that connects areas that have the same temperature

latitude
imaginary lines that run east and west across the Earth and are used to help find locations on the Earth's surface

lava
hot rock that flows out of a live volcano and cools down to form hard rock

longitude
imaginary lines that run from the North Pole down to the South Pole and are used to help find locations on the Earth's surface

Moorish
relating to the people and culture of the North African Muslims that once ruled Spain from 711 to 1492 CE

Renaissance
describes a period that began in Italy in the early 15th century, where artists, scientists and philosophers studied ancient Roman and Greek culture to find new ways to represent and explore the world

transcontinental
something that crosses over into more than one continent, such as the borders of a country or a railway line

Index

Alhambra, the 18
Almería, Spain 13
Alps, the 17, 24
Atomium 18

Baltic states 11
Belgium 6, 8–11, 18, 25
Benelux 11
Berlin Wall 9
bison, European 15
British Isles 10
Budapest 23
buildings, historic 18–19

Caerphilly Castle 18
Champagne 28
cheese 29
chocolate 29
cities, capital 22–23, 27
climate 10, 12–13
cod, Atlantic 14
Colosseum 19
countries (of Europe) 6–7
countries, transcontinental 7
Crkvice, Montenegro 13
culture 26–27
Czech Republic 6, 9, 11, 21
Czechia, see Czech Republic

da Vinci, Leonardo 26
Denmark 6, 9–11, 18–19

Eastern Europe 9–11
energy, sources of 20–21
Equator 5
euro 9
European Union (EU) 9
explorers 4

farming 20–21
First World War 8
fjords 16
food (and drink) 15, 28–29

football 25
forests 14–16
France 6, 8–10, 17, 20–22,
    24–25, 28–29
Franz Josef Land 13
fuels, fossil 21

Gavdos, Greece 13
Germany 4, 6, 8–10, 17, 21, 25, 27
Giant's Causeway 16
Great Belt Bridge 18
Greece 4, 6, 8–9, 13, 18, 25–26, 29
Greenland 10–11

haggis 28
Hagia Sophia 18
ham, Parma 28
Hungary 6, 8–9, 11, 23, 27

industry 18, 20–21
    car industry 21
Ireland 6, 9–10, 16
isotherms 13
Italy 6, 8–9, 17, 19, 24, 26–29

latitude 5
longitude 5
lynx, Iberian 14

manufacturing 20–21
McCool, Finn 16
Mont Blanc 17
Moscow 22
Mount Elbrus 17
Mount Etna 17
mountains 12–13, 16–17, 20

Netherlands, the 6, 8, 10–11, 15,
    25, 29
Nordic countries 11
Northern Europe 10
Norway 6, 10–11, 14, 16, 29

Olympic Games 25

Paris 22, 24
Parthenon 18
Poland 6, 8–9, 11, 15, 25, 29
Pompeii 19

population 6
Portugal 6, 9, 14, 25
Prime Meridian 5
Ptolemy 4

references, grid 5
religion 26–27
Renaissance, the 26
resources, natural 21
rivers 16–17, 22–23, 27
ruskie pierogi 29
Russia 7, 9, 13, 17, 21, 22, 24

Scandinavia 11
Scotland 10, 16, 28
Second World War 9
Shakespeare, William 26
Southern Europe 10
Soviet Union 9, 11
Spain 6, 9, 13–14, 18, 24–25, 29
sport 24–25
Stockholm 5, 23
Strauss, Johann 27
Sweden 6, 9, 10–11, 23
Switzerland 6, 9–10, 17, 25, 29

temperatures, average 13
Tour de France 24
tourism 13, 20–21
trees, olive 14–15
tulips 14–15
Turkey 7–8, 18, 27

UEFA European Championships 25
United Kingdom 5, 6, 9–10, 14,
    18, 24–25

Vatican City 6, 27
volcanoes 16–17, 19

Wales 10, 18
waltz, the 27
Western Europe 10
wildlife 12–15

zones, time 5